Contents

KU-654-136

To the teacher

We have written this book in the hope that it will provide much needed help and guidance to both teachers and pupils in an area of French language learning that is rapidly growing, and likely to grow even more.

There has in particular been a marked shortage of suitable material available for practice, since the Examining Boards have released very little of the material which they have used in examinations. The present book hopes to make good this deficiency. Although the situations included have not themselves been used in examinations, the authors have over ten years' experience of creating such situations to be used in the oral examinations of the Associated Examining Board. The level, format and style of the situations are therefore very close to those of the current examinations. It should be stressed, however, that the views expressed in this book are the authors' own, and are in no way an official statement of Associated Examining Board policy.

In the examinations of most CSE Boards, and at the Basic level of the new GCSE examination as it is at present envisaged, there is no real intervention in the role-play by the examiner; such interventions are the rule, however, in Ordinary level examinations, and will continue to be so at the Higher level of the GCSE: we therefore include suggestions for possible development of each situation along the lines of those provided for examiners. These are, however, only suggestions of possibilities, and since role-play is by definition an activity in which it is the pupil who takes the initiative, the possibilities for development are not only endless but impossible to foresee.

In an examination, of course, the candidate does not see the examiner's instructions. For practice purposes, however, there may be much to be gained from pupils seeing how situations are likely to be developed, and indeed the more able pupils should be able to take that part as well, so that situations can be worked out between pairs of pupils.

The above emphasis on the use of such an activity as role-play in examinations should not, however, blind anyone to the fact that, apart from actually visiting France, role-playing is the nearest one comes to practising French in a real situation, and this is its prime value: it is a valuable, one might say almost indispensable, rehearsal for real life. But since, for the pupils, passing their examinations is also important, it is that aspect we have tended to stress in this book. We hope that both teachers and pupils will find it useful.

TONY WHELPTON
DAPHNE JENKINS

Introduction

Why?

If role-playing appears to be increasing in popularity as far as its inclusion in course-books and examinations is concerned, this is because the learning of foreign languages is increasingly being seen primarily as a means of communication, and the kind of language that is being taught is by and large that which you are most likely to need when visiting the foreign country whose language you are learning.

In other words, it is essentially a matter of rehearsal: of practising for situations which you may very well find yourself having to cope with at some time in the future. Moreover, since when you are abroad you are more likely to be asking questions than answering them, role-play does tend to lay more emphasis on the asking of questions, and the inclusion of role-play in examinations has revealed that this is an area in which traditionally not enough practice has been given.

How to set about it

Let us begin by reminding you of the different ways in which you can ask a simple question.

Imagine that you want to ask a baker if he has any croissants:

1   you can change a statement into a question just by making your voice go up at the end, i.e.
       Vous avez des croissants?
2   you can use the question formula *est-ce que* at the beginning of a statement, i.e.
       Est-ce que vous avez des croissants?
3   you can change the order of the subject and the verb, i.e.
       Avez-vous des croissants?

4   you can add *n'est-ce pas*? to your statement, to mean
    'haven't you?', i.e.
        Vous avez des croissants, n'est-ce pas?

Now your turn!

Give four different ways of asking

1   a hotel receptionist if he or she has any free rooms
2   a passer-by if he or she knows where the Information Office
    is
3   a waiter if he can recommend a good wine.

What do I have to do?

Whatever the situation in which you find yourself, you will be
required to perform one or more of the following:

1   asking for information
2   giving an explanation
3   asking for something
4   paying for something
5   thanking somebody
6   apologising to somebody
7   complaining about something
8   describing something or someone
9   choosing something.

   You will also, of course, have to go through the usual
exchanges of greeting, farewell and so on, and cope with both
face-to-face and telephone conversations.
   You will find that although you may be involved in many
different kinds of situation, the number of questions you actually
have to use is comparatively small. You should make sure that
you are familiar with them all, because unless you are, you are
unlikely to be very successful in making yourself understood in
France.
   Let us look at each of the above categories, or functions, in
turn:

1 Asking for information

Here are some of the more usual questions, words and phrases
you might need:

Est-ce qu'on peut ...?
(e.g. Est-ce qu'on peut prendre le petit déjeuner dans la
chambre?)

Est-ce qu'il ya ...?
(e.g. Est-ce qu'il y a un musée dans cette ville?)

Pouvez-vous me dire ...?
(e.g. Pouvez-vous me dire s'il y a un restaurant près d'ici?)

Pour aller à ...?
(e.g. Pour aller à la piscine, s'il vous plaît?)

Où se trouve ...?
(e.g. Pardon, madame, où se trouve la gare, s'il vous plaît?)

Voulez-vous ...?
(e.g. Voulez-vous me donner un dépliant, s'il vous plaît?)

Avez-vous ...?
(e.g. Avez-vous un plan de la ville?)

Qu'est-ce qu'il y a?
(e.g. Qu'est-ce qu'il y a à faire?)

Depuis quand ...?
(e.g. Depuis quand êtes-vous ici?)

Combien?
(e.g. Combien de kilomètres y a-t-il d'ici à Paris?)

Quel ...?
(e.g. Quelles pêches sont les meilleures?)

Comment?
(e.g. Comment est-il, ton ami?)

Pourquoi?
(e.g. Pourquoi est-ce qu'il n'y a pas d'autobus?)

Qui? (*or Qui est-ce qui?*)
(e.g. Qui est le patron ici? Qui est-ce qui est le patron ici?)

A quelle heure ...?
(e.g. A quelle heure part le train?)

Quand?
(e.g. Quand est-ce que vous arriverez?)

Now your turn!

Try using each of the question forms given above in a different situation from the one given, e.g.

Est-ce qu'on peut visiter le château dimanche matin?

2 Giving an explanation

These are some of the most common verbs you might need, and some of the most common structures:

Devoir
Je dois
Je dois partir demain.

Etre
Je suis
Je suis anglais.

Aller
Je vais
Je vais aller au cinéma ce soir.

Avoir
J'ai
J'ai un sac et deux valises.

Perdre
J'ai perdu
J'ai perdu mon billet.

Avoir besoin
Nous avons besoin
Nous avons besoin d'un garage parce que le pneu
est crevé.

Comprendre
J'ai compris
Je n'ai pas compris ce qu'il a dit.

Avoir peur de
J'ai peur
J'ai peur de manquer le train.

Venir de
Je viens de
Je viens d'arriver en France.

Vouloir
Je voudrais
Je voudrais acheter un cadeau.

Aimer
J'aime
Je n'aime pas la viande trop cuite.

C'est moi qui
C'est moi qui ai téléphoné à la police.

Now your turn!

Try using each of the verbs given above in a different sentence, e.g.

Mon frère doit se coucher de bonne heure parce qu'il n'a que cinq ans.

3 Asking for something

These are some of the most common verbs you might need, and some of the most common structures:

Vouloir
Je veux une chambre à deux lits.
Je voudrais un kilo de poires et un melon.

Désirer
Je désire acheter un jouet.

Avoir besoin de
J'ai besoin de deux kilos de pommes de terre.

Falloir
Il me faut des croissants.

Now your turn!

Try using each of the verbs given above to ask for something different, e.g.

J'ai assez de légumes mais il me faut des poires et des pommes aujourd'hui.

4 Paying for something

These are some of the most common verbs you might need, and some of the most common structures:

Ça fait combien?
Ça fait combien, le gâteau?

Combien coûte . . . ?
Combien coûte le poste de télévision, s'il vous plaît?

Quel est le prix?
Quel est le prix de la voiture?

Devoir
Combien est-ce que je vous dois?

Avoir de la monnaie
Avez-vous de la monnaie?
Je n'ai pas de monnaie.

Voici
Voici un billet de cent francs.

Donner
Je vous donne cinquante centimes.

Etre cher
La viande est trop chère.

Etre bon marché
Les légumes sont bon marché.

Now your turn!

Try using each of the verbs and structures given above in a different sentence, e.g.

Ça fait combien, la robe à manches courtes?

5 Thanking somebody

These are some of the most common verbs you might need, and some of the most common structures:

Merci
Merci bien.
Merci beaucoup.

Remercier (bien, infiniment, mille fois)
Je vous remercie infiniment de votre gentillesse.

Etre gentil
Vous êtes très gentil.

Etre aimable
Vous avez été très aimable.

Now your turn!

Practise using these different ways of thanking someone, e.g.

Les fleurs sont magnifiques. Merci mille fois.

6 Apologising to somebody

These are some of the most common verbs you might need, and some of the most common structures:

Je m'excuse.

Excusez-moi.
Excusez-moi, mais le train est arrivé en retard.

Je vous demande pardon.
Je suis désolé.
Je regrette infiniment.

Now your turn!

Try apologising to someone using the expressions given above, e.g.

J'ai cassé le verre, maman. Excuse-moi, je t'en achèterai un autre.

7   Complaining about something

These are some of the most common verbs you might need, and some of the most common structures:

Ne pas être content (*satisfait*)
Je ne suis pas content parce que les draps sont sales.

Etre fâché
Je suis fâché parce que tu ne m'as pas téléphoné.

Expliquer
Voulez-vous m'expliquer pourquoi le potage est froid, s'il vous plaît?

Plaire
La chambre ne me plaît pas parce qu'elle donne sur la rue.

Ne pas aimer
Je n'aime pas passer une heure à t'attendre.

Now your turn!

Try using the verbs given above to complain about something, e.g.

L'appartement ne me plaît pas parce qu'il est trop petit.

8   Describing something or someone

These are the aspects you might need to describe:

Colour
Il est brun, bleu, blanc, etc.
Il est gris foncé.
Il est gris clair.

Shape
rond
carré
rectangulaire

Size
grand
assez grand
gros
énorme
petit

Material
en cuir (*or* de cuir)
en coton
en laine
en nylon
en tergal

Pattern
uni (= *smooth*)
rayé
à pois
à carreaux

Now your turn!

Use some of the words given above to describe
various objects, e.g.

Je voudrais un complet gris foncé en laine ou en tergal.
Je préférerais un tissu rayé.

9 Choosing something

These are some of the most common verbs you might need, and
some of the most common structures:

Prendre
Je prendrai le plat du jour.

Choisir
Je choisis le tricot bleu plutôt que le vert.

Préférer
Je préfère celui-ci à celui-là.

Aimer mieux
J'aime mieux les raisins que les poires.

Falloir
Il me faut deux timbres.

Valoir mieux
Il vaut mieux prendre le car que le train.

Donner
Donnez-moi 250 grammes de beurre, s'il vous plaît.

Now your turn!

Try using the verbs given in order to choose something, e.g.

Il vaut mieux acheter des timbres au tabac parce qu'on fait la queue au bureau de poste.

10 On the telephone

Here are some phrases which you might meet or need if you are speaking to someone on the telephone:

Allô.
Qui est à l'appareil?
Qui parle?
C'est de la part de qui?
Ne quittez pas.
Est-ce que Pierre est là?
Puis-je parler à Marie, s'il vous plaît?

Now your turn!

Try out some of these expressions by holding an imaginary telephone conversation with a friend.

Preparing a role-play situation

Vocabulary

The vocabulary that you will need in role-playing is the basic vocabulary you have learned throughout your course. As you prepare the situations given in this book, make sure that you revise all the items that you might want to buy in shops, the food and drink you might order in a restaurant, the information you might require at a travel agency or a *Syndicat d'Initiative*, etc. If there is a particular vocabulary item you don't know, try and find a way of expressing the same idea by using different words.

Playing a part

You must also remember that you will be playing a particular part, and although you do not need to be a great actor or actress, you do need to work out the details of your role. Try and imagine that you really are in France, in the situation you have been given, and ask yourself, 'Using the French I know, how can I get this message across?'

Relationship

You must first of all establish what your relationship is with the person to whom you will be speaking. If you are speaking to someone you do not know well, or who is older than you, then the relationship will be a formal one, and you must use 'vous'. But if the other person is a friend, or a member of your family, then the relationship will be an informal one, and you will need to use 'tu'. (And if that kind of situation arose in an examination you would probably lose marks for not using 'tu'.)

Studying the background information

You must always make sure that you are fully aware of all the details of the situation given to you. You might be told, for example, that you are in a restaurant and have only forty francs to spend. In that case, don't be tempted to spend more money than you have. Likewise, if you are told that you have been waiting for a bus for a long time, don't say that you left home five minutes ago.

Conveying the message

The most important thing to remember about conveying the message in each of the four points you have to get across is that you are not being asked to translate from English into French. In fact in examination, most of the instructions are written in such a way that if you try and translate them as they stand, you will get into a mess: you will not be asked to say anything which you have not already learnt during your course, and if there is something you don't know, then either you haven't though about it enough, or you haven't done enough work preparing for your examination.

Often there are several different ways in which you can express the same thing. For example, if you are told to suggest that you visit a museum together, you might say

Si on allait au Louvre?

or

Est-ce que vous voudriez visiter le Louvre?

You might be told to ask the price of a dress in a shop, in which case you could say either

Combien coûte la robe?

Ça fait combien, la robe?

or

Quel est le prix de la robe?

Now your turn!

Find different ways of

1 suggesting that you and a friend go to the cinema
2 asking the price of a green tie.

Developing the situation

If you really were in one of these situations in France, then it is extremely likely that something unexpected might happen. You might find, for instance, that the greengrocer has run out of tomatoes, and asks if you would like something else instead. In an examination you might find the same thing happening, with the examiner intervening in such a way that you have to say something which makes the situation develop. You must think about the possible variations beforehand, and not allow youself to be taken unawares. If you are booking a room in a hotel, for instance, and you have asked for a room with bath on the first floor, you must be prepared to hear that the only room left is a single room with shower on the ground floor. This, after all, is what tends to happen in real life, so you need to practise coping with it before it does happen.

You must listen very carefully all the time to what the other person is saying, and adapt your own role accordingly. Remember that the other person's intervention is giving you further opportunity to express yourself in French, so always say as much as possible. Never restrict yourself to saying just 'oui' or 'non'. Take the initiative and talk.

In an examination, the examiner will have instructions as to how he might try to develop the situation – if the candidate lets him. (If the candidate just ignores what he says, then he will lose marks heavily.) In the practice situations contained in this book, we have given the kind of instructions that the examiner might well have been given for that particular situation; your teacher may want you on occasions to look at that section, or at other times to cover it up so that you have to think it out for yourself.

Overacting

Talking is not the same thing as acting, and although you are playing a part, you should not feel that you have to act as if you were on stage. By all means put your hand in your pocket and pretend to pay a bill, but do not take it any further than that.

Examples of situations

Here are two situations, with an example of how the conversation might possibly go. Obviously, as in real life, someone else might have a totally different conversation based on the same instructions.

Example situation 1

You are in a train, and speak to the person sitting opposite you.

1 Ask whether he/she minds if you open the window.

2 Ask if he/she is going far.

3 Ask if there is a restaurant car on the train.

4 Invite him/her to go with you for a drink.

Fellow passenger

1 Say you don't mind, but it is snowing outside – wouldn't it be better just to turn down the heating?

2 Say you are going to Lyon. Where is he/she going?

   Does he/she live there? It's a long journey, isn't it? Has he/she already eaten?

3 No restaurant car, but a bar which serves drinks.

4 Accept invitation.

How it works

A Est-ce que cela vous dérange si j'ouvre la fenêtre?

B Non, cela ne me dérange pas, mais il neige, n'est-ce pas?
Pourquoi pas simplement baisser le chauffage?

A Je préfère un peu d'air frais. Est-ce que vous allez loin,
monsieur?

B Je vais à Lyon. Et vous, où allez-vous?

A Je vais à Paris.

B Vous y habitez?

A Non, je vais en voyage d'affaires.

B C'est un long voyage, n'est-ce pas? Vous avez déjà mangé?

A Non, je commence à avoir faim. Savez-vous s'il y a un
wagon-restaurant dans ce train?

B Non, il n'y en a pas, mais il y a un bar où on sert des
boissons.

A Ah bon. Avez-vous soif? Voulez-vous venir prendre un verre
avec moi?

B Volontiers. C'est une très bonne idée. Allons-y.

Example situation 2

You are at home, and telephone a French friend called Alain. Alain's brother answers the phone, and tells you that Alain is out.

1   Ask when he will be back.

2   Ask if he received your letter this morning.

3   Ask if he has decided to go out with you this evening.

4   Say you have tickets for a concert and ask if Alain will ring you when he comes in.

Alain's brother

1   Say he has gone to the library, and you don't know when he will be back. Can you take a message?

2   Say you don't think he got a letter today. When was it posted?

3   Say you know he intends to go out this evening, but you don't know who with. Where is he/she thinking of going?

4   Ask for his/her telephone number and if he/she will be at home all afternoon.

How it works

A Quand est-ce qu'il rentrera?

B Il est allé à la bibliothèque et je ne sais pas quand il sera de retour. Est-ce que je peux prendre un message?

A Oui, s'il te plaît. Sais-tu s'il a reçu ma lettre ce matin?

B Je ne le crois pas. Quand l'as-tu postée?

A Hier matin vers dix heures.

B Alors elle arrivera probablement cet après-midi.

A Bon. Je voudrais savoir s'il a décidé de sortir avec moi ce soir.

B Je sais qu'il a l'intention de sortir, mais il ne m'a pas dit avec qui. Où veux-tu aller?

A J'ai deux billets pour un concert et je voudrais y aller avec Alain. Veux-tu lui demander de m'appeler quand il rentrera?

B Bien sûr. Quel est ton numéro de téléphone?

A C'est le 24–16–83.

B Le 24–16–83. Bon. Est-ce que tu seras chez toi tout l'après-midi?

A Oui, j'attendrai son coup de téléphone.

B Je le lui dirai.

A Merci bien et au revoir.

B Au revoir.

Shopping

Situation 1

You go into a boulangerie-pâtisserie, and speak to the shopkeeper.

1 Ask for a large loaf and six croissants.

2 Say you want a plum tart.

3 Ask how much the little cakes in the window are, and buy four.

4 Ask how much it all comes to, and offer a 100F note.

Vocabulary

une tarte aux prunes
  (aux abricots, aux pommes)
la vitrine
un billet de cent francs
une demi-heure
la monnaie

Shopkeeper

1 Say you have just sold the last croissant but there will be more in half an hour.

2 You have only apple tarts and apricot tarts at 18F each.

3 Say the little cakes are 2F 50 each.

4 Say how much it costs and ask if he/she has any change. (Cost is 31F 50 with tart, 13F 50 without.)

Situation 2

You go into a boulangerie-pâtisserie, and speak to the shop assistant.

1   Ask for two loaves of bread.

2   Ask for eight croissants.

3   Say you would like a cake; ask which he/she recommends.

4   Ask how much you owe, and pay.

Vocabulary

un pain
recommander
Combien est-ce que je vous dois?
il reste . . .
un gâteau au chocolat
une tarte aux fruits

Shop assistant

1 Ask what kind of loaves.

2 Say you have only four left. Does he/she want to wait?

3 Suggest chocolate cake or fruit tart. What kind of fruit does he/she prefer?

Would he/she like some small cakes (*babas au rhum*, *tranches à la vanille*, etc.)?

4 Cost is between 10F and 40F, depending on purchases.

Situation 3

You are out shopping and you go into a charcuterie. You speak to the shopkeeper.

1 Ask how much the ham costs, and when he/she has told you, buy half a kilo.

2 Ask which pâté he/she recommends, and buy 250 grams.

3 Order a roast chicken for tomorrow.

4 Apologise for only having a 100F note.

Vocabulary

le jambon
un demi-kilo
un poulet rôti
demain

Shopkeeper

1 Say you have some at 30F a kilo, but the more expensive one is better. When asked, say it is 34F a kilo.

2 Offer various pâtés (*pâté de porc*, *pâté de foie*, *pâté de campagne*, etc.). Recommend the *pâté maison* that you have just made, at 24F a kilo.

3 What weight of chicken? (From two to four kilos.) When will he/she come to collect it?

Say the bill (without chicken) comes to either 21F or 23F.

Situation 4

You are in a clothes shop in France. You have seen a dress (or a shirt) in the window, but you cannot see it in the shop. You have a maximum of 130F to spend. You speak to a sales assistant.

1 Ask about the dress (or the shirt).

2 Ask if you can try it on.

3 Ask if he/she has any belts (or ties) to go with it.

4 Say you prefer one of the belts (or ties) and ask how much it is.

Vocabulary

une robe
une chemise
essayer
une ceinture
une cravate

Sales assistant

1 Ask for exact details of the dress (or shirt).

Say it costs 100F.

2 Would he/she like to try on something else as well? Ask his/her opinion of other items.

3 What kind of belt (leather, synthetic, wide/narrow, colour, etc.) or tie (material, colour, stripes, etc.)?

4 It is 25F, but you have a better one for 35F.

Ask if he/she wishes to buy.

Situation 5

You go into a clothes shop. You have just bought a new jacket and want to buy matching garments. You speak to the sales assistant.

1 Say you want to buy a shirt (or blouse) to match your new jacket, and buy one of those offered.

2 Say you also need a tie (or jumper), and choose one of those offered.

3 Ask if they have any nylon socks (or woollen gloves), and buy two pairs.

4 Ask if they accept cheques or a credit card.

Vocabulary

un veston
une veste
un chemisier
aller avec (= *match*)
un tricot
des chaussettes (*fem.*)
une paire
un chèque
une carte de crédit

Sales assistant

1 Ask the colour and what the jacket is made of, and offer two shirts/blouses, one at 90F, one at 110F.

2 Offer choice of ties at 30F each or jumpers at 80F or 100F.

3 Ask what colour socks or gloves and whether plain or patterned. Offer them at 13F a pair (socks) and 20F a pair (gloves).

4 Present bill and accept cheque or credit card. Bill will range from 146F to 250F, depending on items chosen.

Situation 6

You are a Frenchwoman, Mme Lefèvre. You are in a French market, and go to the stall of a greengrocer you know quite well.

1   Ask how he/she is, and ask about his/her family.

2   Say you want some large onions.

3   Ask for a cauliflower and a cabbage.

4   Buy a kilo of pears.

Vocabulary

la famille
un oignon
un chou-fleur
un chou
une poire

Greengrocer

1 Ask how she likes her new job. Does she have to travel a lot?

2 Are these onions large enough? Recommend some cheaper ones.

3 Offer various sizes and prices. Say the cabbages are not very fresh, but you are expecting some more later on.

 Ask if she would like some fruit today.

4 Tell her the cost: about 23F to 25F, depending on what she has bought.

Situation 7

You are in a supermarket and see a man drop a purse. You try to catch him but he goes out of the shop before you can do so. You look inside the purse and then go to see the manager.

1 Say you saw a man drop the purse.

2 Say that you have opened the purse but there is no name or address in it.

3 Describe the contents of the purse.

Ask what the manager will do if the man doesn't claim the purse.

Vocabulary

le porte-monnaie
laisser tomber
le nom
une adresse
réclamer
rendre

Manager

1 Ask why he/she didn't give it back to the man.

 Ask what the man was like.

2 Ask what is in the purse.

3 Say you will give it to the police, but ask for his/her name and address.

Situation 8

You are visiting some friends for lunch and you want to buy some flowers for your hostess. You go to a florist's shop. You do not want to spend more than 20F.

1 Say you want to buy some flowers.

2 Ask the florist for some advice.

3 Find out the prices and choose some flowers.

4 Buy the flowers, then ask the way to the nearest métro station.

Vocabulary

le conseil
la jonquille
la tulipe
le bouquet
la station de métro
l'arrêt d'autobus

Florist

1   Is it for a present? For someone special?

2   Suggest daffodils or tulips.

3   Large daffodils are 22F a bunch, smaller ones 15F; tulips are 18F a dozen.

    If tulips, ask which colour.

4   It is quite a long way, but there is a bus stop opposite. Where is he/she going?

    The number 10 bus stops near there.

Situation 9

You have arranged to meet a friend outside a big department store in Paris, but arrive early, so you look around the shop. You go to the information desk and speak to a shop assistant.

1 Ask where the toy department is.

2 Ask if you can get there by lift.

3 Ask if there is a café in the shop and if lunch is served there.

4 Ask at what time the shop usually shuts and if there is an evening when it stays open late.

Vocabulary

le rayon des jouets
un ascenseur
au quatrième étage
être en panne

Shop assistant

1 Say that it is on the fourth floor and that there is an excellent choice. What is he/she looking for?

2 Yes, but the lift is out of order. Suggest escalator or stairs.

3 The main café is on the top floor; lunch will be over now, but there is a snack bar on the first floor. Will that do? What does he/she want to eat?

4 The shop usually shuts at 6 p.m. and there is no late evening shopping. Does he/she know the supermarket in the same street? It stays open until 9 p.m. several evenings a week.

Situation 10

You are staying in Paris and you are out shopping. Soon after coming out of a large store you realise that you no longer have your wallet/handbag. You go back into the shop and ask to speak to the manager.

1 Apologise for bothering him/her.

2 Tell him/her about losing your wallet/handbag.

3 Ask what you should do.

4 Ask if he/she thinks there is a chance that it might be found.

Vocabulary

le portefeuille
le sac à main
le gérant/la gérante
déranger
le vendeur/la vendeuse
le poste de police

Manager

1 Say it doesn't matter and ask how you can help.

2 Exactly when and where was the handbag/wallet lost? Which assistant was helping him/her at the time? Has he/she spoken to this assistant about the loss?

Ask what was in the wallet/handbag.

3 Suggest that he/she reports it to the nearest police station. Does he/she know where that is? Give directions.

4 Yes, there is a chance somebody might return it to your office, but there are a lot of thieves about. Does he/she think it might have been stolen, or did he/she drop it?

Suggest he/she comes back the next day.

Situation 11

You go into a grocer's shop, and speak to the grocer.

1 Ask for six slices of ham and a tin of sardines.

2 Say you would like some cheese.

3 Ask him/her to recommend some good wine. Buy two bottles and also a bottle of lemonade.

4 Choose a packet of biscuits and a bar of chocolate.

Vocabulary

une tranche
une boîte de sardines
une bouteille
la limonade
un paquet
une tablette de chocolat

Grocer

1 Thick slices of ham or thin? Portuguese or Breton sardines?

2 Ask what kind of cheese he/she prefers (hard, soft, cream, blue, etc.).

3 What is the wine to go with? Make appropriate suggestions. Wine costs 5F, 9F 50 and 16F.

4 Recommend various kinds of biscuits and chocolate.

   Is that everything? Ask for payment.

Situation 12

You go into a greengrocer's shop in France, but you do not have much money, and you must buy the cheapest fruit and vegetables. You speak to the greengrocer.

1 Buy one cauliflower and a kilo of onions.

2 Ask for the greengrocer's advice on other vegetables.

3 Ask about peaches and pears and decide which fruit to buy.

4 Ask for half a kilo of tomatoes.

Vocabulary

un légume
une pêche
une tomate
un champignon

Greengrocer

1 Large or small cauliflower? Large are 5F, small are 3F 50.
 Spanish onions 4F 50, French 3F.

2 Beans are good value at 2F 80 a kilo, and mushrooms at
 2F 60.

3 Peaches are 4F a kilo, pears 5F a kilo. Suggest apples at 3F
 a kilo.

4 No tomatoes at present; they will arrive later. Would he/she
 like to come back?

 Ask if he/she would like something else. Ask for payment.

Situation 13

You go into a shop, and speak to a shop assistant.

1 Say you were in the shop earlier, and think you left an umbrella behind.

2 Say it was blue and white and not very long.

3 Describe the assistant who served you.

4 Ask if they will let you know if they find it.

Vocabulary

oublier
laisser
un parapluie
faire savoir
servir
le numéro de téléphone

Shop assistant

1 Ask what time he/she was in the shop.

2 Ask who it was who served him/her.

3 Ask if he/she remembers exactly where the umbrella was left.

4 Ask for name, address and telephone number.

Situation 14

You are staying in Paris and have been involved in a slight accident. A jacket (or a dress) that you want to wear this evening has been slightly torn and needs cleaning. You go to a dry cleaner's, and speak to a shop assistant.

1   Say you want the jacket/dress cleaned.

2   Find out when it will be ready.

3   Ask if it can be repaired as well.

4   Ask if it can be delivered to your hotel when it is ready.

Vocabulary

nettoyer
prêt
réparer
livrer
une tache
un supplément
déchirer
urgent

Shop assistant

1   Find out what the stains are and what caused them.

2   It will be ready in two days' time.

   It can only be ready today with extra payment, and even then it might not be ready. But let yourself be persuaded.

3   You do repairs, but clothes have to be sent away, so it won't be back for a few days. The tear is not very serious: suggest that he/she could repair it.

4   You do not normally deliver. Why is it so urgent?

   What time is it needed? Which hotel? As it is so near you can deliver it when you leave work.

Situation 15

You go into a dry cleaner's shop in France, and speak to the assistant.

1 Ask to have your dress/trousers cleaned.

2 Ask when it/they will be ready as you will be leaving the next day.

3 Ask how much it will cost.

4 Ask if clothes can be delivered to your hotel as you will be out all day.

Vocabulary

renverser
descendre à l'hôtel

Assistant

1 Ask what has been spilt on it/them.

2 Explain that the ordinary service takes two days, but there is an express service that takes two hours.

3 The ordinary service is 18F. The express service is 26F. Which will he/she have?

4 Ask which hotel he/she is staying at.

Suggest he/she calls just before closing-time (7p.m.) or early next morning (shop opens at 8 a.m.).

In the restaurant

Situation 16

You are in a restaurant with a friend.

1 Ask your friend if he/she has decided what to eat.

2 Ask what kind of wine he/she would prefer.

3 Ask if he/she has been to this place before.

4 Ask what he/she would like to do later on.

Vocabulary

le vin ordinaire
assez cher
le cinéma
le théâtre
le concert

Friend

1 Say you are not sure. What does he/she think?

Say you don't like what is suggested and suggest something else.

2 Will the house wine do as the other wines are rather expensive?

3 Say you haven't been here before. Has he/she? If yes, was the food good? If not, how did he/she come to hear of it?

4 Would he/she like to go to the cinema? If yes, what kind of film does he/she prefer? If no, what about the theatre or a concert?

Situation 17

You go into a restaurant with a friend who does not speak French. You do not want to spend more than 50F each. You speak to the waiter.

1   Ask if there is a free table.

2   Ask for the menu and for the waiter's advice.

3   Say that that is too expensive and ask how much chicken and chips would cost.

4   Ask waiter to recommend wine.

Vocabulary

libre
la carte
le poulet
les frites (*fem.*)
le plat principal

Waiter

1 Ask for how many people and where they would like to sit.

2 Recommend the *canard à l'orange*. It costs 50F each.

3 Chicken and chips is 45F each.

   Ask if they would like an hors d'œuvre before their main course.

4 Suggest a Muscadet at 20F a bottle, or *ordinaire* at 8F.

   Ask if they would like an apéritif.

Situation 18

You are in a restaurant in France with a friend who does not speak French, so you must order for him/her as well as for yourself. You do not want to spend more than 120F in all. You speak to the waitress.

1 Ask if there is a fixed-price menu.

2 Find out what choice is offered for the cheapest meal.

3 Ask if wine is included and order some.

4 Ask if you will have to wait long, as you are in a hurry.

Vocabulary

le menu à prix fixe
le repas le moins cher
compris
être pressé
le vin en carafe
la carte des vins

Waitress

1 There are two menus, one at 45F and one at 65F.

2 There is a choice of *canard à l'orange*, *bifteck* or *veau*.

   Ask which vegetables they would like.

3 Service is included, but not wine.

   Say the house wine is very good, and give them a wine list.

   Ask which hors d'œuvre they would like (*potage, œufs mayonnaise, crudités*).

4 Say you will serve them straight away.

Situation 19

You are in a restaurant in France with a friend who does not speak French. Neither of you has enjoyed the meal and you send for the manager to express your dissatisfaction.

1 Complain about the meat not being properly cooked.

2 The service was poor; you had to wait too long between courses.

3 The waiter forgot to bring the glass of water you had asked for.

4 There is a mistake in the bill.

Vocabulary

bien cuit
le plat
le verre d'eau
une erreur
une addition

Manager

1 Find out what was ordered and what instructions given.

2 Explain that the waiter is new. Did they tell him they were in a hurry?

3 Apologise about water. Would they like a drink now?

4 Identify the error: the waiter is not used to their prices. Apologise and change bill. Promise better service in future.

Situation 20

You are on holiday in France, but you are the only one in your party who can speak French. You go into a restaurant and speak to the waiter.

1 Ask if they have a table free.

2 Try and get a table on the terrace overlooking the garden.

3 Order the fixed-price meal for everyone.

4 Ask the waiter what he recommends.

Vocabulary

la terrasse
il fait frais
la salle

Waiter

1 Ask how many in the party and where they would like to sit.

2 Say there is one table left on the terrace but it is rather cool outside. Would they prefer an inside table?

3 Say there are three fixed-price meals. Which one would they like?

Ask which starter, main course, vegetables and dessert they would like.

At the hotel

Situation 21

You have just arrived at a hotel in France with your parents and your brother who do not speak French. You speak to the hotel receptionist.

1 Say you want two rooms for one night.

2 Say you would like rooms which look onto the garden and that are near one another.

3 Ask the price of the rooms including breakfast.

4 Ask what time breakfast is served and if you can have it in the bedroom.

Vocabulary

le/la réceptionniste
donner sur le jardin
au rez-de-chaussée
partir
de bon matin

Receptionist

1 For how many people? With bath?

2 Offer one on the ground floor and one on the second floor.

Say there are two together on the first floor, but only one looks onto garden.

3 The rooms are 115F each. Breakfast is 15F extra.

4 Breakfast is from 7.30 to 9.15 a.m. Will they be leaving early?

Situation 22

You are on holiday in France with your family, consisting of
father, mother, a 16-year-old girl and her twin brother. You may
play the part of any member of the family that you choose, but
you are the only one who speaks French. You go into a hotel
and speak to the receptionist.

1   Ask if you can have some rooms.

2   You would prefer rooms with a good view, and not too close
    to the kitchen.

3   Decide whether to accept what you are offered, and ask if
    you can have dinner in the hotel.

4   Ask if there is a lift and if you can have help with your
    luggage.

Vocabulary

une vue
les bagages (*masc.*)
le portier

Receptionist

1 Ask what he/she requires. How many people/rooms? Other requirements (bath/shower)?

2 You have one room on the ground floor (not close to kitchen), and two on the second floor.

3 Dinner is available: what time would they like to eat? Would they like breakfast in their rooms the next morning? At what time?

4 There is a lift. The porter will help. Where is the luggage?

Situation 23

You are staying in a hotel in France and you are the only member of your family who can speak French. Your young brother/sister has been ill during the night. The following morning you speak to the receptionist.

1 Explain the problem.

2 Ask about local doctors.

3 Ask about possibility of changing rooms because of traffic noise.

4 Ask about possibility of providing meals in bedroom.

Vocabulary

se sentir malade
avoir de la fièvre
le médecin
changer de chambre
le bruit
la circulation
le cabinet du médecin
la consultation

Receptionist

1 Express concern and enquire about illness (was it sudden?, possible causes, etc.).

2 Suggest names of doctors. Is boy/girl fit to go to surgery? If so, give times. If not, offer to ask doctor to visit.

3 Say the only room available is on the top floor. Will that do, or will they wait until the next day?

4 Usually only serve breakfast in bedrooms, but can take up lunch and dinner. For mother and father too? What would the patient/they like to eat?

On the telephone

Situation 24

You are at home and telephone a French friend who has been ill.

1 Ask what has been the matter and if he/she is better.

2 Ask if he/she is able to get up now.

3 Ask if there is anything you can do to help.

4 Ask if he/she would like some fruit – grapes or oranges.

Vocabulary

Qu'est-ce que tu as eu?
aller mieux
aider
le raisin
se reposer
un magazine

Friend

1 Say you have had 'flu, but are feeling much better now.

Ask if he/she will come and see you as you can't go out for a few days.

2 You can get up, but you have to rest a lot.

3 Ask him/her to bring you a magazine that you like.

4 You don't feel much like eating fruit, but you would like something to drink.

Situation 25

You telephone a French friend.

1 Apologise for not having turned up to meet him/her yesterday.

2 Suggest meeting on Saturday.

3 Would he/she like to go with you to a party at a friend's house?

4 Arrange details of meeting.

Vocabulary

hier
une surprise-partie
emprunter

Friend

1 Ask what happened.

   Why didn't he/she telephone before?

2 Saturday is difficult. You have a lot to do. What is he/she thinking of doing?

3 Ask for details (when, where, dress, etc.).

4 Agree to go.

   You might be able to borrow your father's car. Would he/she like a lift?

Situation 26

You have been staying in Paris, but have not been well, and this has prevented you from getting in touch with a friend whom you had promised to contact. You now telephone him/her.

1 Apologise and explain why you have not been in touch.

2 Suggest a meeting: give time and place.

3 Suggest where you can go together.

4 You need to buy a good French dictionary, but you do not know where to go to buy it.

Vocabulary

ensemble
un dictionnaire
un manteau
une librairie

Friend

1 Accept apology and ask how he/she is now.

2 You would like to meet but time and place not suitable. Suggest alternative and make arrangements.

3 You need to buy a new coat; will he/she help you choose?

4 Suggest *Le Petit Robert* or *Petit Larousse* and one of the bookshops in the Boulevard Saint-Michel. Say you will take him/her there.

Suggest having a meal together: time depending on arrangements already made. Discuss kind of restaurant you might go to.

Situation 27

You are staying in Paris and you telephone a French friend.

1 Suggest that you meet.

2 Invite him/her out to a meal.

3 Ask him/her to recommend a good restaurant.

4 Choose one of the places recommended and arrange meeting.

Vocabulary

inviter à
être ravi
chinois
vietnamien
le Quartier Latin

Friend

1 You would be delighted, but when and where?

2 Accept, but you are not free on day suggested. Suggest another day.

   Ask whether it is for lunch or dinner.

3 What kind of restaurant has he/she in mind (large, small, French, Chinese)?

   Recommend several restaurants in the Latin Quarter.

4 Ask exactly where he/she is staying.

   Suggest either meeting at Place Monge (at entrance to métro station), or collecting him/her in your car.

Situation 28

It is your birthday and you have received a present of a blouse (or a shirt) from a French friend. You telephone your friend.

1   Express your thanks.

2   Say what you are doing to celebrate your birthday.

3 Ask if you can go and stay with him/her during the summer holidays.

4   Ask about the health of other members of the family.

Vocabulary

un anniversaire
bon anniversaire
célébrer
les grandes vacances
aller (= *to suit*) (Ça te va?)
travailler dur

Friend

1 Wish him/her a happy birthday.

Ask if he/she likes the colour, and if the shirt/blouse suits him/her.

2 Ask what other presents he/she has had.

3 Ask when he/she wants to come and for how long. Explain your own holiday plans.

4 Say they are all well, but your sister is tired as she is working very hard for her exams. Ask about his/her family.

Ask why he/she hasn't written recently.

Situation 29

You are in Paris on your way to stay with some friends in Chartres. Unfortunately your plane was late arriving in Paris, and you have missed the last train to Chartres. You telephone your friends.

1   Ask if anyone has gone to meet you at the station yet.

2   Explain what has happened and apologise for being late.

3   Ask what you should do next.

4   Say you will catch a train the following morning.

Vocabulary

être sur le point de sortir
aller chercher
prendre un train
le vol
retardé
en face de

Friend

1   You were just about to get the car out of the garage. Where is he/she phoning from?

2   Ask why the flight was delayed.

3   When is the next train?

    Has he/she enough money to stay in a hotel?
    If yes, try the large hotel opposite the station.
    If no, would he/she like you to come to Paris by car to pick him/her up?

4   Does he/she know times of trains the next morning?

    Has he/she had a meal? If not, suggest he/she has something to eat.

Situation 30

You are telephoning a friend who lives in Paris.

1 Say you are coming to Paris for a few days and would like to see him/her.

2 Ask how far your hotel in Montmartre is from your friend's house.

3 Suggest that you visit a museum together.

4 Ask about getting to this meeting by bus or métro.

Vocabulary

la semaine prochaine
un musée
en autobus
par le métro

Friend

1 Say you would love to, but will be working during the day, so which day will he/she be free in the evening?

Invite him/her to dinner one evening.

2 Offer to go and fetch him/her by car.

3 Ask what he/she would like to see most, and suggest museum accordingly.

4 If bus, suggest métro might be quicker and cheaper. If métro, suggest bus might be more interesting.

Ask time and place of meeting.

At the garage

Situation 31

You are in your parents' car in France, but your parents cannot speak French. You stop at a petrol station, and speak to the petrol pump attendant.

1 Ask for some petrol, and ask him/her to check the oil and the tyre pressure.

2 Ask how far it is to the nearest town.

3 Ask if you can buy cigarettes and sweets here.

4 Ask how much it is, and if you can pay by credit card.

Vocabulary

l'essence (*fem.*)
le super
l'ordinaire (*masc.*)
l'huile (*fem.*)
un demi-litre
vérifier
la pression des pneus
les bonbons (*masc.*)
la carte de crédit

Pump attendant

1   Ask what kind of petrol and how much.

Tell him/her that the car needs half a litre of oil, but the tyres don't need any air.

2   It is about 20 km, but if they are looking for somewhere to have lunch, there is a good restaurant in a village about 5 km away.

3   Say yes, and ask what he/she would like.

4   Work out price at 4F a litre and 8F for oil, plus cigarettes and sweets.

Situation 32

You are on a motoring holiday in France, but are the only one in your party to speak French. You go to a petrol station, and speak to a petrol pump attendant.

1 Buy petrol and get oil checked.

2 Ask where the toilet is.

3 Ask if one can buy sweets and drinks for the children.

4 Ask what there is to see and do in the nearest town.

Vocabulary

les toilettes (*fem.*)
à l'arrière
une boisson
la ville la plus proche
un bâtiment
l'équitation (*fem.*)
la natation
la piscine

Pump attendant

1 Ask how much petrol and what kind.

2 The toilet is at the back: first door on the left.

3 Say there are no hot drinks; what cold drinks would they like?

   There are no sweets left; they will have to go to the nearest town for sweets.

4 What kind of places do they like to visit? Depending on answer, suggest: old buildings, churches, market place, etc. What kind of activities do they prefer? Depending on answer, suggest: swimming pool, park, horse-riding, etc.

   Ask where they come from and how long they are staying.

   If necessary, ask to be paid for petrol and drinks.

In the street

Situation 33

You have witnessed an accident, and you approach a policeman who has just arrived.

1 Say that it was you who telephoned the police.

2 Tell him that you saw what happened.

3 Say that you were standing at the bus stop when a little boy ran out in the road in front of a car.

4 Say that you shouted to try and stop him.

Vocabulary

téléphoner à la police
ce qui s'est passé
devant
crier
empêcher
un coup de téléphone

Policeman

1 Ask his/her name and address.

2 Ask what happened.

3 Ask why the car did not stop more quickly.

4 Ask if he/she knows the little boy and where he lives.

Thank him/her and ask for telephone number. Ask when he/she will be at home to receive a call.

Situation 34

You are in town, and in the street you see a friend whom you have not seen for some time. You go over and speak to him/her.

1 Ask how he/she is, and how his/her family are.

2 Ask why he/she hasn't been to see you for so long.

3 Suggest meeting soon.

4 Ask if he/she has time to come and have a quick drink with you now.

Vocabulary

être occupé
prendre un verre
avoir le temps

Friend

1 Say you are all well; what about his/her family?

2 Say you have been very busy with your new job. Why didn't he/she phone?

3 Accept, but where and when? Make suggestions if necessary (e.g. cinema, café).

4 Accept, but ask where you can go, as you haven't much time to spare.

Situation 35

You have just arrived in France on holiday when your car breaks down about 50 km from the coast. Another motorist stops, and you go and speak to him/her.

1 Say that you have broken down, but you don't know what is wrong.

2 Ask for help in changing the wheel as you have never done it before.

3 Ask if he/she knows a good restaurant nearby.

4 Thank him/her for helping, and offer to take him/her to a café for a drink.

Vocabulary

tomber en panne
ce qui ne va pas
changer la roue
un pneu crevé (une crevaison)
le pneu arrière
un outil

Motorist

1 Say you think there is a puncture in one of the rear tyres.

2 Ask where the spare tyre and the tools are kept.

3 Say there is a good restaurant called 'Chez Pierre' in the next village, about 2 km further on.

  Ask how much further he/she has to drive today.

4 Say you live nearby, and invite him/her to your house for a drink instead.

Situation 36

You are in Paris, and you want to go to the Rue de Rivoli. You are on foot, and you ask a passer-by for advice.

1   You ask the best way to get there: on foot, by bus, or by métro?

2   Ask how long it will take.

3   Choose a means of transport and ask for directions.

4   Repeat the directions. Say thank you, and ask if he/she knows the shops in the Rue de Rivoli.

Vocabulary

à pied
s'intéresser à
le parfum
le cadeau

Passer-by

1 Say it depends whether he/she is in a hurry. It is quite a nice walk, but it is quicker by bus or métro.

2 Ten minutes by métro, a quarter of an hour by bus.

3 If bus: bus stop is opposite book shop just down the road. If métro: métro station is first left, then second right.

4 Say you know them fairly well, and ask what kind of shops he/she is interested in.

   Say the shops there are mostly small and expensive: good for buying perfume, presents, etc.

Situation 37

You are staying in Paris, and have arranged to visit a friend living in the Joinville district of Paris. You have been waiting for a bus for a long time, but no bus has come. You approach a passer-by, and engage him/her in conversation.

1 Ask why there are no buses.

2 You are in a hurry. Ask how else you can get there.

3 Find out where the nearest phone box is so that you can ring your friend.

4 You do not know your friend's phone number. How can you find out?

Vocabulary

en grève
la cabine téléphonique
l'annuaire des téléphones (*masc.*)

Passer-by

1 The buses are on strike today. How long has he/she been waiting?

2 Suggest taxi or métro, but the métro station is rather a long way away.

   Find out exactly where he/she is going and what time he/she is due to arrive there.

3 There is no phone box in this street, but he/she could try the nearby café.

4 Ascertain if he/she knows name and address of friend. Tell him/her to look in phone directory or ask someone in café to help.

At the railway station

Situation 38

You are on your way to stay with a French family in Poitiers. You have just arrived at the railway station in Poitiers, and there is no-one at the station to meet you. You telephone the family and one of your pen-friend's parents answers the phone.

1 Say you have just arrived at the station.

2 You caught the 8 o'clock train as you arrived in Paris earlier than expected.

3 You tried to ring from Paris, but no-one answered.

4 How do you get to their house?

Vocabulary

venir de (+ *infinitive*)
plus tôt
faire des courses
reconnaître
porter

Father/mother

1 Express surprise at early arrival and ask for an explanation.

2 Why hadn't he/she let you know?

3 Nobody answered as you had all gone shopping.

4 Say you will come and fetch him/her in the car. How will you be able to recognise him/her? What is he/she wearing? Where will you find him/her?

Did he/she have a good journey?

What has he/she had to eat? Would he/she like to go into the cafeteria to have a drink as it will take you a quarter of an hour to get there.

Situation 39

You are at the taxi rank at a railway station in Paris. You have a lot of luggage, and want to go to Charles de Gaulle Airport to catch the 9.30 a.m. plane to London. You speak to a taxi-driver.

1   Ask the taxi-driver if he is free.

2   Say you haven't much time to spare, and how long will it take?

3   Ask him to help you with your luggage.

4   Say you have to be in London before lunch in order to meet your parents.

Vocabulary

un chauffeur de taxi
l'Aéroport Charles de Gaulle (*masc.*)
Londres
à l'heure

Taxi-driver

1 Say yes and ask where he/she wants to go.

2 Say it depends on the traffic, but you usually do it in about half an hour.

Ask what time is the flight.

3 Ask which suitcases belong to him/her.

Comment on weight of cases, and ask how long he/she has been staying in Paris.

4 Ask if there is another flight that morning.

Say you will do your best to arrive in time.

At the travel agency

Situation 40

You are a French person. You are in Le Havre and you want to go to Reims with your children aged nine and three. You visit a travel agency to enquire about the journey and, if possible, to buy your tickets. You speak to the travel agent.

1 Ask if it is possible to travel by train.

   If it is, ask if you need to change trains, and if there is an alternative means of transport.

2 Ask how long the journey will take, and about departure times.

3 Ask how much it will cost and buy your tickets.

Vocabulary

par le train
voyager
changer de train
le moyen de transport
les heures de départ (*fem.*)
un aller simple
un aller et retour
demi-tarif

Travel agent

1 Say it is possible, but there is no direct service.

   Say there is a direct coach service. Which would he/she prefer?

2 By train it takes four hours. There are several trains a day to Paris. By coach it takes six hours, but there is only one coach a day, and it leaves at 10 a.m.

3 Ask how many travelling, and age of children. Single or return?

   If train, under four travel free. First or second class? Fares: first class 120F single, second class 85F. Return is double, children pay half.
   If coach, fares: 70F single. Return double, children over three pay half.

   Does he/she want to buy tickets now? Arrange payment.

Situation 41

You are spending your summer holiday in Poitiers, but decide you would like to spend a few days at the seaside. You go to a travel agency to make enquiries, and speak to the travel agent.

1 Ask which are the best seaside resorts near to Poitiers.

2 Ask about different kinds of accommodation there.

3 Ask about the cheapest and quickest way of getting there.

4 Make arrangements for your journey.

Vocabulary

une station balnéaire
le logement
une plage de sable
une pension

Travel agent

1 Does he/she want a large sandy beach (Royan or Les Sables d'Olonne) or an interesting town like La Rochelle, with access to the Ile de Ré?

2 Does he/she want a hotel, boarding house, camp site, etc?

Depending upon which chosen, ask for more detailed requirements: number in party, length of stay, etc., and offer to book.

3 Train is fastest: direct to La Rochelle. Coach is cheaper but slower.

What day and time does he/she want to travel?

At the Syndicat d'Initiative

Situation 42

You have just arrived in a French town, and you go to the
Syndicat d'Initiative **for information. You speak to an employee.**

1 Ask for help in finding a hotel.

2 Ask what there is to do and see in the region.

3 Ask if there is a restaurant in the hotel and whether there
are good restaurants in the town.

4 Ask if there is a cinema in the town.

Vocabulary

la région
le confort
la durée
le séjour
la piscine

Employee

1 Ask what kind of hotel: price, comfort, length of stay, number in party.

 Recommend l'Hôtel Bel Air.

2 Ask what he/she is interested in, then suggest anything suitable – museum, swimming, etc.

3 Offer a list of restaurants in the town.

4 Say there is no cinema here, only in the next town, which is 6 km away. Has he/she a car? If not there are plenty of buses.

 Wish him/her a good stay.

Situation 43

You are visiting France with your family: you have a young child, and do not want too expensive a holiday. On arriving at a seaside town, you go to the *Syndicat d'Initiative* and speak to an employee.

1 Ask if you can have a plan of the town.

2 Ask for a list of hotels and some advice about the best places to stay.

3 Ask where the best shops are, and where the best restaurants are.

4 Ask about interesting places to visit and things to do.

Vocabulary

un plan de la ville
la liste des hôtels
trois étoiles
pension complète
demi-pension
le centre commercial
le quartier
pittoresque

Employee

1   Would he/she like a simple plan of the town which costs
    nothing, or a map of the region, including town plan, which
    costs 4F?

2   Offer a hotel list. What are their requirements (three-star,
    two-star, one-star, etc., full/half board, near the sea, etc)?

    Offer to telephone and make booking.

3   What kind of shops (supermarket outside town, new
    hypermarket with smart shops, old picturesque quarter with
    small shops, etc.)?

    What kind of restaurant do they want?

    Suggest beach activities. How old is child? Possibility of
    'Club Mickey' on the beach; boat excursions, sailing, tennis.
    In town: museum, gardens, cinema. Château a few
    kilometres away. Is information required about any of these?

Situation 44

You are on holiday in France with your family, including your elderly aunt. You go to a seaside town on the South-west coast and call at the *Syndicat d'Initiative*. You speak to an employee at the enquiry desk.

1 Ask about the availability of hotel accommodation.

2 Say that a lift is essential because of your aunt.

3 Ask them to telephone to make a booking for you.

4 Ask about restaurants in the locality.

Vocabulary

réserver
un ascenseur
une tante
la montagne

Employee

1 Find out how many in party, length of stay, how they are travelling.

Ask what kind of accommodation required: full/half board, bath, shower, etc.

2 Ask what grade of hotel required: only two-star hotels and above have lifts.

Do they want a view of the sea or of the mountains? In town or out of town?

3 You agree to telephone, but explain that some hotels may be full. Would they mind being separated, either on different floors of the same hotel or in different hotels?

4 Either offer a list of restaurants or recommend several different restaurants.

At the airport

Situation 45

It is 2.30 p.m. You have arrived at Marseille airport and had arranged to meet a friend there arriving from Paris. You go to the information desk and speak to the clerk.

1 Ask what time the flight from Paris is due to arrive.

2 Ask what time coaches leave the airport to go to the city centre.

3 Ask if there has been a message for you.

4 Thank him/her and ask where coaches leave from.

Vocabulary

le vol
un autocar
le centre de la ville
un message
le hall

Clerk

1 Say flight should arrive at 2.45 p.m. but it will be one hour late.

2 Coaches to city centre run every half hour.

3 Ask his/her name. Yes, there is a message. When asked, say friend doesn't want him/her to wait, but will get in touch later to suggest new rendez-vous.

4 Near entrance in main hall. Can he/she see the stop?

Situation 46

You are at a large Paris airport, waiting to catch a plane back home to London. You hear an announcement, but cannot understand it. You decide to ask another passenger waiting near you if he or she can explain.

1 Say that you could not understand the announcement. It was too fast.

2 Say that you are afraid of missing your plane.

3 Say that someone has told you that it is foggy in London, and that your flight will probably be delayed.

4 Ask if he/she will tell you when the departure time of your flight is announced.

Vocabulary

une annonce
manquer
le vol
retardé
faire du brouillard
l'heure du départ

Passenger

1   Say that announcement was for passengers to Holland. Is
    that where he/she is going?

2   Which flight does he/she want to catch?

3   Say that you have just heard that the fog has cleared. Is the
    weather often bad in London?

    Does he/she live in London? If not, where?

    You will be staying in the centre of London. How can you get
    there from Heathrow Airport?

4   Ask about his/her stay in France. What did he/she enjoy
    most?

At customs

Situation 47

You are going through customs on the way home from a holiday. You speak to a customs officer.

1 Say that you have nothing to declare.

2 Ask why you are having to wait so long, as you have a train to catch.

3 Ask whether he/she wants to look inside your suitcases.

4 Say that the case he/she is looking at is not yours.

Vocabulary

déclarer
la valise
à l'étranger
vérifier
un bagage
un appareil photo
appartenir

Customs officer

1 Didn't he/she buy anything abroad?

2 There is a lot of luggage to check. How many pieces of luggage has he/she?

3 Ask him/her to open a suitcase. Why are there five cameras in this suitcase?

4 Ask why he/she was carrying it if it does not belong to him/her.

   Ask his/her name and ask him/her to go with you.

Situation 48

During a long holiday in France, you go to Spain for a few days, and on returning to France, where you will be staying for another month, you go through the French customs, and speak to a customs officer.

1 Declare what you have bought in Spain.

2 Say where and when you bought your camera before going to Spain.

3 Ask how much you will have to pay for your extra bottles of wine.

4 Ask if you can pick up your suitcases and leave.

Vocabulary

l'Espagne (*fem.*)
le tabac
le vin
le parfum
la montre
le droit de douane
la bouteille

Customs officer

1 Ask if that is everything, mentioning anything that may have been forgotten – wine, perfume, tobacco, etc.

2 Check that the watch he/she is wearing is not new.

3 Say the duty will be 4F a bottle. Ask how many bottles.

4 Check on which luggage belongs to him/her before allowing to pass.

At the camp site

Situation 49

You are camping in France with your family, and your younger sister falls ill. The doctor arrives, and as you are the only member of the family who speaks French, you speak to the doctor.

1 Say your sister is feeling unwell.

2 Say you think it is something she ate yesterday.

3 Say she slept very badly last night, and she seems feverish.

4 Say your parents are very worried, and ask if you should go back home.

Vocabulary

se sentir malade
avoir de la fièvre
prendre la température
inquiet
rentrer
avoir mal
grave
descendre à l'hôtel

Doctor

1 Ask what the trouble is. Has she a pain, and if so, where?

2 Ask what she had to eat yesterday, and if she has eaten anything today.

3 Ask if she has had her temperature taken.

Ask how old she is and if she is often ill.

4 Say that it isn't necessary to go home. It's nothing serious, but she needs rest. Could they perhaps stay in a hotel?

Situation 50

You are on holiday in France with your family, and you are the only one who speaks French. You have just arrived at a camp site, and you go into the camp office, and speak to the employee there.

1 Say who you are, and that you have booked for a week.

2 Ask where you can put up your tent.

3 Ask if you can buy fresh bread and milk on the site.

4 Ask where the toilets and showers are.

Vocabulary

réserver un emplacement
dresser une tente
la douche
la camionnette

Employee

1 Check on how booking was made, and on people in family.

2 Say that it isn't far, and that you will accompany them.

3 Say there is milk in camp shop, and baker's van visits site at 8 o'clock every morning. Ask if he/she would prefer to shop at the nearest supermarket. If so, does he/she know where it is?

4 Toilets and showers are 25 metres away, on the right.

Is there anything else they want to know?

At the post office

Situation 51

While on holiday in France, you go into a post office, and speak to the counter clerk.

1   Ask how much the postage is to England.

2   Ask for four stamps, and ask how long it takes for a letter to get to England.

3   Say that you have a parcel to send to England.

4   Ask if you can borrow a pen to fill in the form, and ask how much it costs.

Vocabulary

un timbre
un paquet
remplir
une fiche
la douane
emprunter
une carte postale
le contenu
la valeur

Counter clerk

1 Ask whether it is for letters or postcards. Tell him/her the different rates.

2 Say a letter takes only a few days, but a postcard takes about a week.

3 Ask about the contents and value of the parcel, and ask him/her to fill in a form for the customs.

4 Say the parcel plus stamps costs 29F 50.

Situation 52

You are travelling in France, and have arranged for your family to send letters for you to collect at the local post office. You go to the post office, and speak to the counter clerk.

1 Ask whether there is any mail for you.

2 Ask whether there will be another delivery today as you are expecting another letter.

3 Buy stamps for the letters and postcards you have to post.

4 You have a parcel to post.

Vocabulary

le courrier
une pièce d'identité
une livraison
attendre
revenir

Counter clerk

1 Ask what name. There is one letter. Ask for identification.

2 There will be another delivery later in the day. Ask if he/she can call back.

Ask how long he/she will be staying.

3 How many letters? How many postcards? Where are they going to?

4 Where is the parcel going? There is a customs declaration to fill in if it is going out of the country. What is in the parcel, and what is its value?

At the police station

Situation 53

You are staying with a family in France. You have lost your purse, but are not sure where you have lost it. You go to the local police station and speak to a policeman.

1 Ask if he can help you as you have lost your purse.

2 Give a description of the purse and its contents (money and air ticket to London).

3 Say that you have to go back to England in a few days' time and don't know what to do.

4 Ask what you should do about your lost air ticket.

Vocabulary

perdre
un porte-monnaie
un billet d'avion
le bureau des objets trouvés

Policeman

1 Ask where and when it was lost.

2 Ask what enquiries have been made so far, i.e. shops, transport, etc.

3 Suggest he/she goes to the lost property office.

Ask for details of the French family as they could send the purse on to England if it is found.

4 Suggest he/she telephones the airport to explain about the air ticket.

Say that you will do your best to find the purse, but you are not very hopeful.

Situation 54

You are staying in Paris when you discover that you have lost your wallet which contained nearly all your money. You go to the police station to report your loss, and speak to a policeman.

1 Tell him about losing your wallet.

2 Say you have lost nearly all your money and that you don't know what to do.

   Ask him if he has any suggestions to make.

3 Say that you will have to go home sooner than you had intended.

Vocabulary

un portefeuille
suggérer
proposer
un passeport
l'Ambassade britannique
un chéquier
un chèque de voyage
une agence de voyage
l'assurance (*fem.*)

Policeman

1 Sympathise and find out exactly when and where it was lost, and what he/she has done about it. Establish contents of wallet.

2 Has he/she still got passport and airline tickets? If yes, say there should be no problem. If no, suggest he/she contact British Embassy and airline.

 Ask if he/she has a credit card or a cheque book, or any traveller's cheques. If yes, suggest going to a bank. If no, suggest phoning family or contacting British Embassy.

3 Ask if insured. If so, suggest going to travel agency to make claim.

Staying with a French family

Situation 55

**You are staying with a French family by the name of Bernard.
You go into the kitchen and speak to M. or Mme Bernard.**

1 Ask if you can help with the washing up.

2 Say that you are enjoying your stay very much and hope
that he/she isn't too tired with the extra work.

3 Say that you want to go and buy something in town. Is there
anything he/she needs from the shops?

4 Ask what time you need to be back for lunch.

Vocabulary

aider
faire la vaisselle
le torchon
le séjour
en ville

M./Mme Bernard

1 Thank him/her. Does he/she know where the tea towel is?
  What does he/she do to help at home?

2 You're not too tired, and it's a pleasure having him/her.
  Would he/she like to come again next year?

3 Does he/she know where the baker's is, as you would like
  some bread and cakes.

4 Lunch is at 12.30 p.m. Don't be late, as you will be going out
  in the car later. Would he/she like to come?

Situation 56

You are in France, staying with a French family. They have all gone out, leaving you alone, as you wanted to write a letter. The telephone rings and you answer it.

1 Ask who it is.

2 Say where everybody has gone.

3 Ask if you can take a message, or if the caller would prefer to ring back.

4 Say what time the family will probably be back.

Vocabulary

rappeler
un projet

Caller

1   Say it is M. or Mme Layard, and ask to speak to M. or Mme Piquet.

   Ask who is speaking.

2   Ask why he/she has been left alone in the house.

3   Ask if he/she knows what the family has planned for Saturday evening, as you would like to invite them for dinner. Would he/she like to come too?

4   Ask if he/she is enjoying the stay, and how much longer he/she will be in France.

   Will he/she ask M. or Mme Piquet to phone when they come back?

Situation 57

You have been staying with a French family, and would like to buy them a present before you go home. You discuss this with a friend.

1   Ask if he/she has any ideas about a suitable present.

2   Say you have 30F to spend.

3   Find out where the best shops are.

4   Ask if he/she will come and help you choose something.

Vocabulary

dépenser
délicieux
le jouet
le jeu
le grand magasin

Friend

1 Ask if they all like chocolates. If yes, say you know where to buy delicious chocolates. If no, suggest flowers, or toys for the children. What do they like to play with?

2 Say little cars and some games are not expensive.

3 The best shops are the department stores in the town centre. When will he/she have time to go there?

4 Agree, but you can only manage a lunch hour. Will that be all right? If so, arrange to meet.

At the bank

Situation 58

You are in a bank in France, and speak to the bank clerk.

1 Ask if you can change some English money into French francs.

2 Ask what is the rate of exchange.

3 Ask if you can use your credit card in France.

4 Ask where the cash desk is.

Vocabulary

le taux de change
une pièce d'identité
la caisse
faire la queue
en argent comptant

Bank clerk

1 He/she can change money if he/she has proof of identity.

2 Give the current rate. How much does he/she want to change?

3 In many places it is possible: look for the sign. But it is often cheaper to pay cash.

4 On his/her right, where there is a queue.

Ask how long he/she is staying in France, what visits he/she has made, etc.

At home

Situation 59

You are a French boy or girl. You go into the living-room at home, where your father/mother is working, and speak to him/her.

1 Say that you are going to see a friend.

2 Say that if anyone phones you will be at Sylvie's house.

3 Ask what time dinner will be ready.

4 Ask what is for dinner.

Vocabulary

prêt
le poulet
un légume

Friend

1 Ask if parents agreed to send money, and when he/she thinks it will arrive.

2 Agree to lend some. Ask how much is needed.

You will need to go to the bank to draw out money. How soon does he/she need it?

3 Ask why he/she didn't bring more money. Where has all his/her money gone?

4 Say he/she must not worry, and need not repay you straight away.

How will he/she repay parents for the extra money they will be sending?

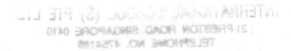

Role-play practice French

Tony Whelpton

Chief Examiner in French, The Associated Examining Board

Daphne Jenkins

Assistant French Teacher, Pate's Grammar School, Cheltenham
Senior Assistant Examiner, The Associated Examining Board

Longman

LONGMAN GROUP UK LIMITED
Longman House
Burnt Mill, Harlow, Essex CM20 2JE, England
and Associated Companies throughout the world

First published 1986
Eleventh impression 1994

Set in 10/12pt Linotron Helvetica Roman

Produced through Longman Malaysia, PA

ISBN 0-582-22444-6

By the same authors
In your own words: French
La boîte aux lettres
Comprenez-vous?
Let's get it right: French
Opinions: Book, Transcript, Cassettes
Le Monde en face
Visa 1: Pupil's Book, Teacher's Book
Visa 2: Pupil's Book, Teacher's Book
In the same series
Role-play practice: German